Program Authors

Diane August	Jan Hasbrouck
Donald R. Bear	Margaret Kilgo
Janice A. Dole	Jay McTighe
Jana Echevarria	Scott G. Paris
Douglas Fisher	Timothy Shanahan
David Francis	Josefina V. Tinajero
Vicki Gibson	

Mc
Graw
Hill
Education

Cover and Title pages: Nathan Love

www.mheonline.com/readingwonders

Send all inquiries to:
McGraw-Hill Education
2 Penn Plaza
New York, NY 10121

ISBN: 978-0-07-679192-7
MHID: 0-07-679192-0

Printed in the United States of America.

2 3 4 5 6 7 8 9 RMN 20 19 18 17 16

A

Unit 3 Going Places

The Big Idea: What can you learn by going to different places?

Week 1 · Rules to Go By 4

Phonics: *Ii* 6

Words to Know: *to* 7

Can I Pat It? Fiction 8

Tim Can Tip It Fiction 14

Writing and Grammar: Narrative Text 20

Week 2 · Sounds Around Us 22

Phonics: *Nn* 24

Words to Know: *and* 25

Nat and Tip Fiction 26

Tim and Nan Nonfiction 32

Writing and Grammar: Informative Text 38

Week 3 · The Places We Go 40

Phonics: *Cc* 42

Words to Know: *go* 43

We Go to See Nan Fiction 44

Can We Go? Nonfiction 50

Writing and Grammar: Narrative Text 56

(t) Laura Ovresat; (c) Danielle D. Hughson/Flickr/Getty Images; (b) Gaia Bordicchia

Essential Question

What rules do we follow in different places?

Go Digital!

4

Let's Play Ball!

Talk About It

How are the children following rules?

Ii

Say the name of each picture.

Read each word.

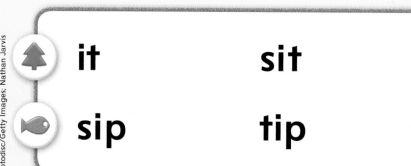

| it | sit | pit |
| sip | tip | Tim |

to

We need **to** sit.

It is good **to** listen.

7

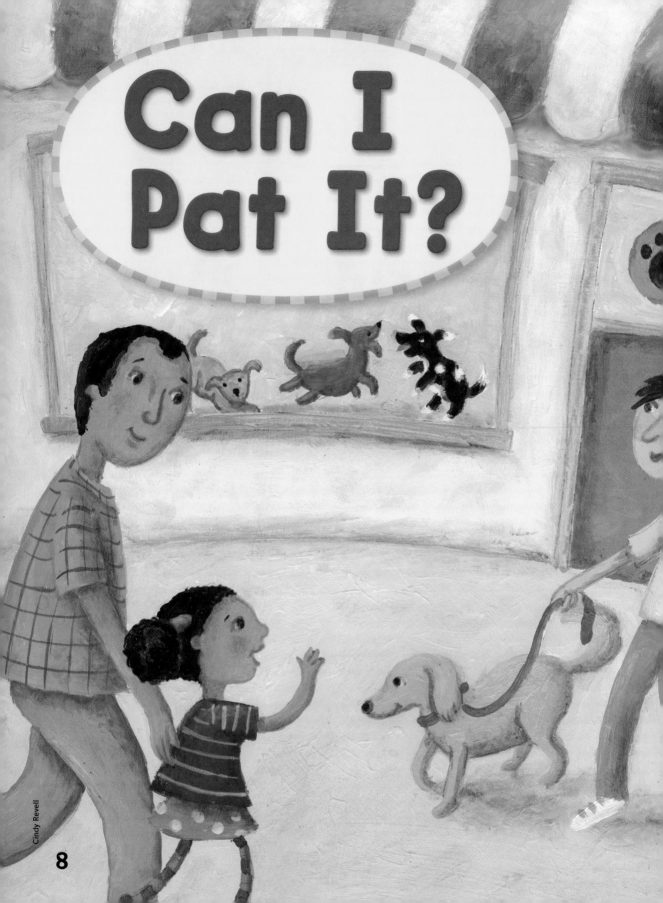

Can I Pat It?

Cindy Revell

I like **to** pat it.

Cindy Revell

Can I pat it?

I like to pat it.

I like it.

Can I pat it?

Tim Can Tip It

14

Tim can tip the .
pail

Laura Orresat

Tim can tip the .

bag

Tim can see the  tap.

bird

Tim can see the tap.

cat

Tim can sit **to** pat the .
cat

Write About the Text

Pages 8–13

Leo

I answered the prompt: **Write a new story, using "Can I Pat It?" as a model.**

Student Model: *Narrative Text*

Pattern
I asked a question as in the story.

Can I eat it?

I like to eat it.

I like the carrot.

Grammar

The **sentence** ends with a **period.**

Can I eat it?

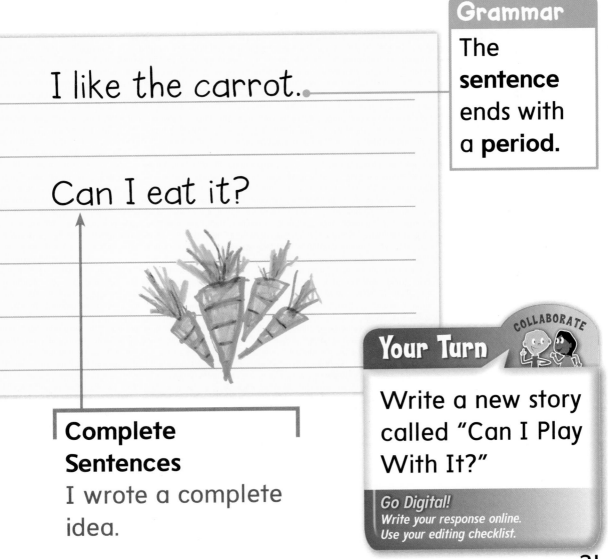

Complete Sentences

I wrote a complete idea.

Your Turn COLLABORATE

Write a new story called "Can I Play With It?"

Go Digital!
Write your response online.
Use your editing checklist.

21

Essential Question
What are the different sounds we hear?

Go Digital!

Keep Your Ears Open!

 **Talk About It**

What sounds do these instruments make?

Nn

Say the name of each picture.

Read each word.

Nan	**nap**	**tin**
man	**Nat**	**pan**

and

Nan **and** I hear a splash.

I see **and** hear a bird.

25

Nat and Tip

Julia Seal

Nat **and** Tip like the .

ball

Nat and Tip like to sip.

Nat and Tip see the .

children

Julia Seal

Nat and Tip  the .
hear hammer

Julia Seal

Nat and Tip  the !

hear

dog

Julia Seal

Tim and Nan

Tim **and** Nan  the  .

hear   hen

33

Tim and Nan  the .

hear   tractor

Tim and Nan see the  corn.

35

Tim and Nan see the  barn .

oink, oink

Tim and Nan the .

hear   pig

Write About the Text

Nat and Tip

Pages 26-31

Amelia

I looked at pages 26 to 27. I answered the question: **What sounds might Nat and Tip hear around them? How do you know?**

Student Model: *Informative Text*

Clues
I used details in the picture to tell Nat is speaking.

Tip hears Nat talk.

Nat hears a bird sing.

Details

I wrote a sentence about something else they hear.

Nat and Tip hear a ball go whoosh.

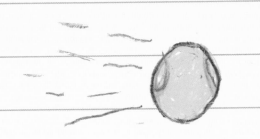

Your Turn

COLLABORATE

Look at pages 29 to 31. If you were at the park with Nat and Tip, what sounds would you hear? Use text evidence.

Go Digital!
Write your response online.
Use your editing checklist.

Essential Question

What places do you go to during the week?

Go Digital!

COLLABORATE

Talk About It

Why is this boy at this place?

Jose Luis Pelaez/Blend Images/Getty Images

Let's Go!

Cc

Say the name of each picture.

Read each word.

 cat　　　　**cap**　　　　**can**

Read Together

go

Mom and I **go** to the store.

We **go** to see the cat.

We Go to See Nan

Gaia Bordicchia

Cam and I **go** to see Nan.

Cam can pat the cat.

We can see the .
book

Cam can go and sit.

The cat and I go and sit.

Can We Go?

Can we **go** to the ?
library

We can go in a .

taxi

Can we go to the  ?

market

We can go in a .

bus

We can go, go, go!

Write About the Text

Pages 44–49

Sara

I responded to the prompt: **Write a journal entry from the boy's point of view. Tell about his day at the bookshop.**

Student Model: *Narrative Text*

We go to see Nan.

Grammar

The **sentence** begins with a **capital** letter.

Cam sees a cat.

We get books to read.

Setting

I used the picture to tell about his day.

Your Turn

Write a journal entry from the girl's point of view.

Go Digital!
Write your response online.
Use your editing checklist.